D1543396

THE
COMPLETE
GERANIUM

THE
COMPLETE
GERANIUM

*Cultivation, Cooking
and Crafts*

SUSAN CONDER

POTTER

Published by Clarkson N. Potter, Inc., distributed by Crown Publishers, Inc.,
201 East 50th Street, New York, New York 10022

CLARKSON N. POTTER, POTTER and colophon are trademarks of
Clarkson N. Potter, Inc.

Conceived and produced by Breslich & Foss, London
Copyright © Breslich & Foss 1992
Text © Susan Conder 1992

All rights reserved. No part of this book may be reproduced in
any form or by any means, electronic or mechanical, including
photocopying, recording, or by any information storage and
retrieval system, without permission in writing from the
publisher.

Printed in Great Britain
Consultant: Dr Maria Lis-Balchin
Designer: Roger Daniels
Illustrator: Marilyn Leader

Library of Congress Cataloging-in-Publication Data

Conder, Susan.
The complete geranium: cultivation, cooking, crafts/Susan
Conder, – 1st ed.
p. cm.
1. Pelargoniums.   2. Geraniums.   3. Pelargoniums—Utilization.
4. Geraniums—Utilization.   I. Title.
SB413.G35C66   1992
635.9′33216—dc20

ISBN 0-517-58883-8
10 9 8 7 6 5 4 3 2 1
First Edition

CONTENTS

Preface

Technically, this book is not about geraniums, but about pelargoniums. These popular tender perennials are closely related to geraniums, which are hardy herbaceous perennials, much used as permanent planting in beds and borders and as ground cover. The name 'geranium', however, is what most people call pelargoniums, and though technically incorrect, the name still stands. Thus, the familiar pink or red flowered houseplant is not a geranium at all, but actually a pelargonium. Since even serious gardeners and nurseries have accepted the misnomer, we, too, will try to keep things simple by referring to the plants not by their official Latin name, but by their common name: geraniums. The technical differences between geraniums and pelargoniums are explained in more detail in the Appendix.

S.C.

True geraniums include both garden and wild flowers, such as the Geranium sanguineum *(Bloody Cranesbill) shown above. The scarlet pelargoniums opposite are what are commonly known as geraniums.*

INTRODUCTION

Geraniums are South African in origin and the earliest known variety in Europe was grown in the seventeenth-century garden of the famous English plant collector, John Tradescant. Later, in 1700, we know that the Dutch Governor of Cape Town sent a particular species to Holland and thereafter more and more species were gradually introduced. Francis Masson, a Scots horticulturalist, risked his life at the behest of King George III to introduce some 50 new species from the Cape. (He was later to go missing in the freezing North American winter of 1805, presumed frozen to death, in pursuit of yet more new plants.) Geraniums reached the U.S., possibly via the West Indies, in the mid to late eighteenth century.

Geraniums have had peaks and troughs of popularity. They were ubiquitous in the beginning of the nineteenth century and during the late Victorian period, when they were cultivated in their thousands, by nurserymen and avid enthusiasts. Whole greenhouses were devoted exclusively to raising geraniums, as they were to the raising of many other genera, such as *Petunia*, *Dian-thus* and *Camellia*, which caught the Victorians' fancy. In his turn-of-the century book, *Greenhouse Management for Amateurs*, the British author, W. J. May, laments:

> The varieties [of geraniums] amount to several hundreds and it is much to be regretted that they are so multiplied, for in many cases they are so much alike that it is quite impossible to tell them apart. Scarlets, indeed, are so numerous that it is difficult to distinguish them by name at all, except in the case of a very few sorts, which are really distinct.

Geraniums fell out of favour during and between the two World Wars, due partly to the high cost or unavailability of fuel for heating greenhouses. It was only in the second half of this century that they began to regain their popularity.

Hybridization of geraniums has always been a subject of interest. In Victorian times, when the process of pollination was first understood through the use of the microscope, amateurs and professionals alike were eager to create new hybrids. Young ladies would hang nosegays of

William Midwood's painting, 'His Favourite Blooms', shows the universal popularity of zonal geraniums during the Victorian era.

especially lovely geraniums upside down, over their own plants, hoping to achieve cross pollination. It was not unusual for geraniums to be sent from private homes to nurseries for cross pollination, rather like dogs or horses being sent to stud.

This interest still remains strong. About forty years ago, a Professor Craig of Pennsylvania State University succeeded in breeding the modern, seed-raised strains which are so popular today. Some thirty years ago, again in America, Miss Frances Hartsook bred the Unique hybrids; a few years later in England, the Reverend Stringer introduced the long-flowering, double-flowered Deacon, or floribunda strain; and in Australia, Ted Both introduced the Stellar, or Staph strain.

Ongoing developments include the pursuit of a wider colour range, including pure yellows, although creamy yellows, such as the double zonal 'Creamery', tinged with pale yellow, are already available. Other goals of hybridizers include seed-raised strains of double-flowered forms of ivy-leaf and zonal geraniums, and regals with more compact growth habit and shorter flowering stalks. They are also seeking improved resistance to disease.

Today geraniums are popular the world over and as well as the old-time favourites – the scarlet zonals for bedding and window boxes, the ivy-leaved types for hanging baskets and the regals for showy, sumptuous blooms – there is increasing interest in less usual forms, including miniatures, ideal for patio gardening, and the scented-leaved types with their subtle beauty. This book aims to cover the familiar and the unusual, the traditional and the innovative, and provide a wealth of growing tips and display ideas, whatever the size of your garden.

TYPES OF GERANIUMS

Once you start to explore the different types of geraniums you will be amazed at the choice available, from exotic, showy blooms to scented-leaved varieties grown mainly for their fragrant foliage.

Most people are familiar with the top dozen or so zonal, ivy-leaved and regal types, usually sold by garden centres and flower shops, but there are many others, some with great charm and subtle beauty. If you wish to discover a wider range of geraniums, you may have to visit specialist nurseries, a few of which are listed in the Appendix. Geranium or pelargonium clubs and societies are also good sources of more exotic or unusual plants, with exchanges of seed and cuttings among the 'perks' for members.

The main forms are described in the following pages. Each form has many different varieties and some of these are listed in the Appendix. The best way to appreciate the range of plants and to make your personal choice is, of course, to see them 'in the flesh' but the following should give you an idea of what to look for.

ZONAL GERANIUMS

The most familiar geraniums, such as the ubiquitous red-flowered houseplant, are known as zonal, or garden, geraniums, named for the dark ring, or zone, that is often found on the leaves. Zonal geraniums are easy to care for and cultivate and bloom for months. They make bushy plants, usually growing to a height of 30–60cm (1–2ft), and are popular both in pots and window boxes and as formal bedding plants. If left as

Zonal geraniums, such as the white-eyed, pink 'Dagata' (above), the single white 'White Orbit' (above right), and the pink 'Cherry Blossom' (right) are equally suitable for the garden, greenhouse, conservatory or house, and in pots or the open ground.

permanent planting in frost-free areas, they have been known to grow as high as 1.5m (5ft) tall. Young growth is fleshy and semi-succulent but the stems become woody with age, especially in hot climates.

The large round flower heads, known as 'umbels', can grow up to six inches in diameter. Each umbel is made up of anywhere from five to 200 tiny individual florets. These florets come in three forms: single, with only a few petals, semi-double, with up to eight petals, and double, with nine or more. Naturally, the doubles, with so many layers of petals, produce umbels of the densest, richest colour, but many people prefer the subtle elegance of the single flower.

Zonal geraniums come in an extraordinary array of colours. Aside from the familiar red, white or pink varieties, there are vibrant scarlets, crimsons and magentas or more muted tones like cream, apricot or pale lavender. Particularly lovely are the bicoloured flowers, where the petals can be either edged, speckled or softly suffused with a contrasting colour. Most zonal geraniums bloom from early summer to early autumn, but if they are kept under glass at 13°C (55°F) or warmer, they can continue to flower all year round, providing a welcome reminder of summer in the cold winter months.

Garden centres tend to carry a limited range of the most popular and showy zonal forms, perhaps offering only one white, one pink, one scarlet cultivar, and so on, and their plant labels can be infuriatingly short of information, but there are several types of zonal geraniums, each with its own character.

The zonal geranium 'Red Elite' makes attractive summer bedding.

Dwarf and miniature types

Dwarf and miniature zonals were developed after WWII, to meet the need for small plants to grow in the then new, smaller homes and greenhouses. Technically, miniatures are a maximum of 12.5cm (5in) high from the soil to the top of the foliage, and dwarfs are no more than 20cm (8in) high. Flowers can be single, semi-double or double, and come in the same colours as the full-sized zonals. Some carry diminutive flower heads, others carry relatively large trusses. The leaves can be plain green, gold or heavily zoned, but many have dark leaves, having been bred from the nearly black-leaved Victorian varieties, 'Salmon Black Vesuvius' and 'Red Black Vesuvius'.

Dwarf and miniature types are slightly harder to grow than ordinary zonals, but, given adequate light and a temperature of 13°C (55°F), they can bloom all winter.

The dwarf zonal geranium 'Emma Hossler' carries large double blooms on compact plants.

Ornamental-leaved types

Just when a variety's beauty of leaf becomes more valuable than its flower is a matter of conjecture, but many zonals are grown for their exceptionally attractive leaves, and in some cases the flowers are actually removed. Ornamental-leaved types are often listed separately in plant catalogues, as coloured-leaved, fancy-leaved or variegated-leaved geraniums or pelargoniums. The leaves can be a single colour, such as bronzy black, pale green or gold; bicolour, including green and white, bronze and green, green and cream, or bronze and gold; or tricolour, in

'Little Dorrit', a bicolour zonal, makes attractive summer ground cover.

various shades or tints of green, white, cream, yellow, and red or reddy brown. The central colour can have a slight division, or 'butterfly marking', or consist of a solid, enlarged zone.

Ornamental-leaved forms are generally less vigorous than other zonals, and need careful feeding, watering and lighting. Intensity of colour can vary according to intensity of light and feeding; low light levels, as in winter, and too much feeding, especially of nitrogenous fertilizer, can cause leaves to become less vivid and more green. On the other hand, too much light can cause the leaves to scorch and fade.

Occasional reversions may occur, with

The tricolour zonal geranium 'Mrs Pollock' is a traditional favourite for bedding schemes.

all-green shoots appearing on a variegated or coloured-leaved plant. Remove these shoots to prevent them overwhelming the weaker, coloured or variegated ones. Some forms are difficult to propagate, and therefore relatively expensive.

The variegated 'Mrs Quilter' displays the typical leaf markings of zonal types.

Unusual Zonals

As well as the popular zonal geraniums, there are many unusual types which you will probably only find at specialist nurseries. These include Irene, Deacon, Rosebud, Cactus-flowered and Stellar types, which are described briefly here.

The robust, strong-stemmed, naturally bushy Irene varieties are American in origin, and ideal for bedding. They have lush foliage and large, long-lasting, semi-double or double flowers on stiff stalks. Because of their vigorous growth habit, they need generous feeding and watering.

'Irene Genie', like all Irene types, makes a bushy, robust plant.

'Apple Blossom', a rosebud geranium, needs protection from the rain for its double blooms.

Deacon, or floribunda, varieties were the result of crossing a miniature zonal with an ivy-leaved cultivar. Most are dwarf, bushy and compact, but if grown in generous-sized containers, they respond by growing relatively large. They carry prolific double flowers, starting earlier in the season than other zonals, and need generous feeding.

Rosebud, or noisette, forms were developed in the nineteenth century. They have tight double blooms, so densely packed with petals that they cannot open fully, creating a rosebud effect. To prevent the plants from growing lanky, they should be frequently pinched out.

Deacon varieties, such as 'Deacon Romance', are long flowering, with double blooms.

'Spitfire' has the narrow-petalled flowers typical of cactus-flowered geraniums.

Cactus-flowered types, called poinsettia geraniums in America, have single or double flowers with twisted, pointed, quilled petals. These plants can also get lanky if not regularly pinched out.

Stellar types are Australian in origin, and have flowers with dainty, quilled petals, the top two forked, the lower ones serrated. If the dense, star-shaped foliage is not thinned periodically, the centre of the plant may grow mouldy.

F_1 and F_2 hybrid seed strains

F_1 hybrids are a relatively new development, first appearing commercially in America in the 1960s. The seed strains are obtained by crossing two closely related cultivars. Hybrids have several advantages: quick and reliable germination, disease resistance, immaculate uniformity of height, growth habit and early flowering time, and the ability to flower within four months of sowing under glass, given a temperature of 21°C (70°F).

Since F_1 hybrids have to be grown from new seeds annually, there is no need to worry about over-wintering or taking cuttings; unfortunately, they are somewhat expensive and the varieties available are limited. With their simple appearance, they are ideal in bedding-out schemes. F_2, or open-pollinated, hybrids are less expensive than the F_1 but also less reliable.

IVY-LEAVED GERANIUMS

These leathery, waxy-leaved plants are also known as trailing, cascade, hanging or basket geraniums. These are derived from *P. peltatum*, so called from the peltate, or shield-like, lobed leaf, which also resembles ivy, hence its common name. They form trailing plants, usually under 90cm (3ft) long, but up to 4.5m (15ft) grown as permanent plants in mild conditions. Their stems are brittle and not usually free branching; frequent pinching out from an early age encourages dense growth. They are usually grown in window boxes or hanging baskets, but can also be used as ground cover or

'Summer Showers', an ivy-leaved strain, has a range of complementary colours.

trained against walls, indoors or out, or up pergolas.

The flowers are single, semi-double or densely double, and are more limited in colour range than zonals, with mauves and pinks predominating and true reds and purples rare. They flower from early summer until early autumn, and are less likely to flower out of season than the zonals. They are relatively greedy, of both water and food, but are otherwise easy to care for. As with the zonals there are miniature and dwarf forms which are similar to the type but scaled down.

A more unusual ivy-leaved form was developed in the 1970s, by grafting 'Rouletta', a red-and-white striped cultivar, with other ivy-leaved forms. This produced hybrids having characteristics of both the rootstock and the scion, or named, variety.

One of the Harlequin series, developed by grafting the striped 'Rouletta' with other ivy-leaved forms.

REGAL PELARGONIUMS

Regal pelargoniums are the grandest and most dramatic flowers in the geranium family. Also known as show, fancy, grandiflora or decorative pelargoniums, and in America as Lady or Martha Washington pelargoniums, they have unzoned, slightly furry, serrated leaves and huge, showy flowers. Regals were so-called because many of them had their nineteenth-century origins in the royal greenhouses of Sandringham, Norfolk, England.

The flower trusses contain fewer but larger blooms than the zonals, each trumpet-shaped floret growing up to 5cm (2in) across. Most are single, although each floret can have more than five petals, and their ruffled, fringed or frilly edges create the impression of double blooms. The colour range includes white, pink, salmon, mauve, crimson, scarlet, orange, violet and near black – all but true blue and yellow. Many are bicoloured with richly contrasting tints, veins or blotches.

'Black Knight' has single, rich maroon flowers, edged in a fine white line.

'Mrs Hickman', like all regal types, has delicate blooms and performs best under glass.

The flowering period is from late spring to early summer, with a second, smaller flush in late summer if the plants are dead-headed. Some modern cultivars, however, are repeat flowering, well into winter.

The plants are bushy, growing 45–60cm (18–24in) high and wide, but can become substantial, 90cm (3ft) or more high, in their second year of growth. Regals are more suitable for growing as house or greenhouse plants than in the open garden, where their relatively short flowering period and vulnerable blooms make them less successful than zonals. Named varieties are grown from cuttings.

'High Fidelity' displays the contrasting petal markings typical of regals.

Miniature, dwarf, or angel types

Angels are classed as miniature or dwarf regals, the name probably derived from 'Angeline', a nineteenth-century dwarf cultivar no longer in existence. Known as pansy-faced geraniums in America, in fact they bear little resemblance to regals, one of their many parents. All have single, five-petalled flowers, mostly in the mauve colour range, often marked with a deeper colour. They are compact, usually under 30cm (12in) high, and outstandingly free and long flowering.

SCENTED-LEAVED TYPES

With the increased demand for foliage plants, scented-leaved geraniums have become more widely available. Many are species, collected from the wild, while others are hybrids. The foliage ranges from modest to attractive and is scented or, more technically, aromatic. Originally nature's device to repel foraging animals, the scent of most cultivated forms is pleasant and includes lemon, apple, orange, peppermint, pine, rose and other less well-defined aromas. The leaves vary from huge to tiny, solid to deeply lobed or lacy, shiny or mat or velvety, and some are variegated. The flowers of most types are small, mauve with darker markings, unscented and sometimes sparse, but they can have a modest charm and elegance.

'Lady Plymouth' has rose-scented, variegated leaves.

'Prince of Orange' has an upright growth habit and orange-scented foliage.

Most scented-leaved geraniums make upright, eventually woody plants, 45–90cm (18–36in) high, less across. They are usually grown as house or conservatory plants, but are ideal for planting in containers out-doors, where they can be brushed or touched in passing to release their scent. The lists on page 61 give details of the various scents used in cooking.

UNIQUE TYPES

These large, shrubby, slender, upright woody plants have leaves that are often deeply lobed and scented, sometimes pleas-antly but often unpleasantly. These hybrids have regal-type flowers but a more compact growth habit and greater tolerance of high temperatures and direct sun.

'Unique Claret Rock' makes an upright, woody-stemmed plant with aromatic leaves.

GERANIUMS IN THE GARDEN

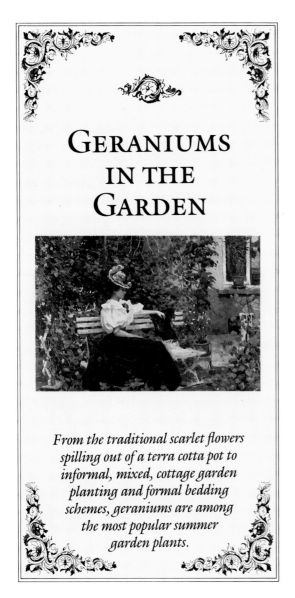

From the traditional scarlet flowers spilling out of a terra cotta pot to informal, mixed, cottage garden planting and formal bedding schemes, geraniums are among the most popular summer garden plants.

Geraniums are as diverse in their decorative use outdoors as they are in their forms, colours and growth habits. Though they are frost tender, which usually limits their flowering season in cool temperate climates to four months from late spring until early autumn, they can create glorious effects over that period, used both in traditional and more informal, imaginative ways.

Large-scale formal bedding and edging are now restricted mainly to public parks and gardens; in ordinary gardens geraniums are more often tucked informally into the overall scheme, either in open ground or in attractive containers.

The chapter on Looking after Geraniums (see pages 72–83) describes in detail the conditions – basically sun and well-drained, fertile soil – that geraniums prefer. This chapter deals with the aesthetic, 'fun' side: using geraniums on their own or with other flowers to create a range of delightful effects.

THE MOST SUITABLE TYPES

While any geranium will benefit from a brief period outdoors in the summer, where exposure to the sun ripens the wood and makes the plant healthier and haler, it is wise to keep in mind which situations are most appropriate for each type of geranium. For example, formal outdoor beds require plants with long flowering periods and

good weather resistance, like zonals. Regals, which are more delicate, should be grown on sheltered, sunny patios, where their flowers are protected from the wind and rain. They are wonderful mixed with other plants in giant pots or tubs. Although their huge, vibrant blossoms are short-lived, the foliage of the regals will continue to provide

Cascades of ivy-leaved geraniums tumbling over a sun-drenched wall create a colourful, Mediterranean look.

an excellent muted background for other flowers.

Zonal geraniums, with their almost machined uniformity and huge 'lollipop' flowers, are perfect for formal bedding, but would look out of place in a herb or wild garden, where fragrant-leaved species and cultivars, with their modest appearance and small flowers, are ideal.

Cultivars with single or semi-double flowers are generally better for outdoor use, especially bedding, than double-flowered or Rosebud forms, because water gets trapped in densely packed petals, and rot sets in, while single and semi-double forms shed water more easily. Single- and semi-double flowers also tend to be self cleaning, dropping faded petals, while double flowers must be deadheaded, or the faded blooms become eyesores.

These pink and mauve ivy-leaved geraniums create a harmonious effect against a simple, rustic, white-washed wall.

WORKING WITH COLOUR

Colour in the garden is a matter of personal taste, but certain guidelines tend to produce generally pleasing results. Dark, solid backgrounds, such as yew hedges, tend to show up pale or white-flowered geraniums to advantage. Whitewashed walls, white-painted fences and even the silvery white foliage of plants such as *Helichrysum petiolare* set off dark-coloured geraniums to advantage.

Red or orange brick walls or paving demand careful consideration, since they can look strident with scarlet or crimson geraniums. Whether used formally or informally, groups of a single cultivar have greater impact, seen from a distance across a garden, than groups of mixed colours. Up close, however, such as the area around a seating area or on a patio, subtle variations in colour can be appreciated. Here, you might combine all-pink cultivars with white-flowered, pink-edged types; pale, mid- and deep pink cultivars or other subtle variations on a theme.

Lastly, although geraniums are most loved for their warm, traditional pinks and reds, white-flowered cultivars open the field for combinations that wouldn't work in the normal colour range of geraniums: white geraniums can be combined with the oranges and yellows of nasturtiums and French and African marigolds or pot marigolds, for example, or the icy cool combination of white ivy-leaved or zonal varieties with purple petunias, dark blue lobelias, blue ageratum and silver-leaved *Senecio cineraria*.

GERANIUMS IN CONTAINERS

Container growing is where geraniums excel. Options range from single pots of zonal geraniums, hung in wire rings or brackets fixed to house or garden walls, to window boxes, hanging baskets and large tubs or urns with geraniums as part of mixed planting.

Zonals and ivy-leaved types are most popular for container growing, but scented-leaved types are valuable for their cooling, soothing contrast to stridently bright flowers and, especially in window boxes, their fragrance can be enjoyed both inside and out. Those scented-leaved types with a lax habit can enhance hanging baskets or urns, as an unusual alternative to ivy-leaved types.

If you mass containerized geraniums, whether on their own or combined with other plants, the result always has more impact than the sum of the parts. Even in entirely paved gardens, it is possible to create a lush, jungly effect. Containerized plants displayed in horizontal tiers on reproduction Victorian wirework plant stands can make dense walls of colour. Much the same effect can be achieved by arranging rows of potted geraniums, shortest in the front, tallest at the back, in the Victorian bedding-out fashion. The paved area under a window box filled with ivy-leaved geraniums could be fitted with a bench, and the ground and bench covered with potted geraniums and other summery plants such as tuberous-rooted and wax begonias, blue pansies, busy lizzies and fuchsias.

Small pots clustered around a large one can be especially effective. For example, a standard oleander in a large pot or tub could create the focal point for smaller pots of ivy-leaved and scented geraniums, regals, *Helichrysum petiolare*, variegated agaves and tender echeverias.

Lastly, an old-fashioned variation on the containerized theme is to sink geraniums, still in their containers, into the ground, for summer display. This is particularly suitable for regals, which can be put out before flowering and returned to the house or greenhouse afterwards. This system is simple and convenient and helps prevent the growth of excessively lush foliage at the expense of flowers, which can occur on very rich soils.

Ornate wrought-iron balconies or verandahs make perfect showcases for geraniums, whether trained along a railing or suspended in hanging baskets.

There is a wide variety of containers available. Although the orange-brown of traditional terra cotta pots is unsympathetic to many of the pinks and reds of geranium flowers, terra cotta is so much a part of the visual language of gardens that it doesn't matter. White-painted Versailles tubs, bleached wooden beer barrel halves and stone and reproduction stone urns are traditional and also work well in terms of colour. The recent influx of glazed Oriental garden pots, including lovely deep inky blue-blacks, stone-greys and water blue-greens, increases the options.

Above: *Stone urns on pedestals are ideal for ivy-leaved geraniums. Here nearby petunias repeat the colour scheme.*

Right: *Simple Oriental glazed pots make handsome partners for geraniums, and come in a range of colours.*

PLANT PARTNERS FOR GERANIUMS

There are so many plants which associate well with geraniums that it is almost easier to eliminate first the few that don't. Annuals or tender perennials with equally rigid, vertical growth habits, such as celosia, also called Prince of Wales' feather, scarlet salvia,

calceolaria, French and African marigold and canna, all tend to emphasize the rigidity and less-than-graceful form of zonal types. Although they were popular combinations in Victorian bedding schemes, and would be historically accurate, nowadays the preference is for plants that fill the area around and between geraniums with a soft, horizontal mass of flowers and/or foliage.

Trailing lobelias are perhaps the most popular filler in pots of zonal types, and are equally good in hanging baskets with ivy-leaved geraniums. As well as the pale and deep blue varieties, there are rich violet types, ideal with dark purple geraniums, such as the ivy-leaved, nearly black-flowered 'Rio Grande' or the regal 'Cezanne'.

While lobelia always plays 'second fiddle' to geranium, geranium and fuchsia have a more competitive relationship, being of roughly equal size and visual weight. They can look striking together, with trailing fuchsias partnered by upright geraniums, and ivy-leaved geraniums partnered by upright fuchsias. The range of flower colours is similar, although the pure orange scarlets of geraniums are rare among the fuchsias. The partnership is a cultivational compromise, since fuchsias prefer more shade, water and humidity than geraniums, but it generally works. Petunias are the third member of this trio, capable of trailing when planted round the edge of a hanging basket, or growing upright when given adequate space.

Marguerites, now technically *Leucanthemum* cultivars, are sold in various sizes and shapes. Tiny dwarf types can be used as edging round a large central geranium; large (and expensive) standards can form the focal point of a pot, around which ivy-leaved geraniums are planted.

Regal and ivy-leaved geraniums, verbena and helichrysm fill an urn in an informal scheme, and blend well with the spires of acanthus and wine-red clematis.

The trailing, half-hardy *Helichrysum petiolare*, with its graceful lax stems of rounded, soft grey leaves, is an ideal partner for all geraniums, both in colour and form. Several cultivars are available: 'Limelight', or 'Aureum', with soft, lime-green leaves; 'Variegatum', variegated silver and white; and 'Microphyllum', with diminutive foliage, but slightly temperamental.

A favourite Victorian partner for geraniums, is what they called germander speedwell or Neopolitan violets, and is today called ground ivy, correctly *Glechoma hederacea* 'Variegata'. This trailing, mat-forming plant, with tiny lavender flowers and evergreen, pale green leaves splashed with white, is particularly good in window boxes and hanging baskets, where its waterfall effect is seen to best advantage. Where flower colours allow, the nasturtium's graceful trailing stems and round leaves are a good antidote to the rigidity of zonals.

An unusual partner from a similar South African origin is the cheerful Livingstone daisy, *Mesembryanthemum criniflorum*, with much the same hot red, pink and salmon colour range. Like the geranium, it thrives in full sun and can tolerate drought, but needs bright sun to open its daisy-like blooms.

Another idea is to pair geraniums with permanent plants in large containers. Use geraniums, especially the ivy-leaved types,

to edge pots filled with standard bays, *Cordyline australis*, *Phormium tenax*, *Yucca* species and cultivars, and any palms. If there is no room actually in the pot, cluster smaller pots of geraniums round a central, large tub. In window boxes, a row of dwarf, topiary box 'balls' makes a good central feature, surrounded by ivy-leaved geraniums.

Above: *The fountain-like growth habit of* Cordyline australis *makes it a superb focal point, with regal and zonal geraniums, ivy and lobelia in supporting roles.*

Above left: *No window can fail to look charming wreathed in delicate pink flowers. Geraniums trained against a wall can reach a great size and require little maintenance.*

The more different the types of plants you combine with geraniums (or indeed, with each other), the less formal the effect, since much of formality is to do with calm repetition. On the other hand, the 'one of each' approach can result in a confused, 'shopping list' appearance. Nonetheless, a glorious medley of, for example, geraniums with fuchsias, marguerites, variegated ivy, lobelias and variegated dwarf euonymus, or with tuberous-rooted begonias, hebes, variegated × *Fatshedera lizei* and busy Lizzie, given thoughtful colour control and juxtaposition, could be outrageously wonderful. The inclusion of a few flowering tobacco plants in a mixed display is always welcome for their scent which, unlike that of scented-leaved geraniums, does not need to be touched or bruised to be released. And, if their rigidity can be obscured, African marigolds can be included for their 'companion planting' ability to deter whitefly – especially useful with regals.

If you prefer a calmer approach, repeated hanging baskets containing the same ivy-leaved cultivar and *Helichrysum petiolare* can be fixed at equal intervals along a balcony, on the columns of an open porch or wall. With balconies, you have the added option of using the entire structure as a sort of giant hanging basket, by allowing pots or floor-level window boxes of ivy-leaved geraniums to trail between the railings.

GERANIUMS FOR FORMAL BEDDING SCHEMES

In a formal bedding scheme, one type of zonal cultivar is normally grown per bed, with the plants spaced 30–45cm (12–18in) apart, according to vigour, in each direction. Most traditional of all, and supremely Victorian in connotation, are scarlet geraniums, with their perpetual gaiety. In his

Trailing perennials, such as periwinkle, ivy or variegated ground ivy, add another dimension to geraniums along a balcony or raised wall.

Rustic Adornments for Homes of Taste (1856), the Victorian author Shirley Hibberd wrote: 'Among showy plants, the scarlet geraniums may take the first place as bedders, for their foliage is as fresh and hardy as their blooms are brilliant and continuous'. Traditional choices are 'Paul Crampel' with single scarlet blooms and bright green clearly zoned leaves, or 'Gustav Emich', with bright red, semi-double blooms; for many years the latter have appeared in beds outside London's Buckingham Palace.

Seed-raised, F_1 hybrid strains are often used as bedding now, since they are cheaper to raise, but many older zonal cultivars have a good record as bedding. These include 'Irene Genie' and 'Irene Toyon', with semi-double, coral-pink and bright, crimson-red flowers, respectively, and the semi-double, salmon-pink, 'King of Denmark'. 'Maxim Kovaleski', an old, vermilion-coloured cultivar, is especially weather resistant and free flowering. Deacon hybrids (see page 16), with their sturdy, floriferous habit are also good bedding plants.

Variegated foliage bedding schemes are another option. The pink-flowered, tricolour zonal 'Mrs Henry Cox', also sold as 'Mr Henry Cox' and 'Henry Cox', with its green, brilliant gold, deep red and black leaves, is traditional. However, it and other tricolour types are relatively slow growing, and cuttings take a year to reach planting-out size, which is costly in terms both of space and expense. Then, too, some people find the tricolours, especially when seen en masse, rather frenzied in appearance.

White-edged, green-leaved cultivars, such as the elegant, tall red-flowered 'Caroline Schmidt' or the pale-pink 'Chelsea Gem', combine the liveliness of variegated foliage with quick growth and are perhaps more soothing to the eye. Solid, golden-leaved cultivars, such as the old 'Verona', with pure golden yellow foliage and single, rose-pink flowers, and 'Golden Crest', with yellow leaves and single orange flowers, offer a more subdued warmth and colour than the highly contrasting variegation.

Formal Victorian geranium beds some-

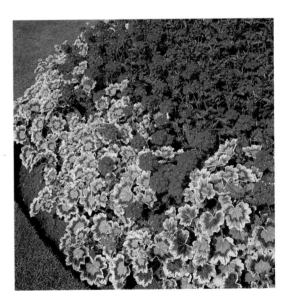

The tricoloured leaves of these massed zonal geraniums make a striking contrast with their red blooms.

This display of zonal geraniums is a superb example of formal summer bedding.

times contained several different cultivars of graded heights, from the shortest, planted as edging, to the tallest placed in the middle of an all-round bed or the back of a front-facing one. The cultivars they favoured, such as the scarlet dwarf 'Tom Thumb' and 'Mrs Ricketts', the white-eyed scarlet nosegay type 'Duchess of Kent' and the variegated 'Flower of the Day', are no longer grown, but the idea could be interpreted in

modern cultivars or F_1 hybrids, including the dwarf and miniature varieties.

In traditional formal bedding, occasional 'dot plants' (called 'eye-catchers' in Victorian American gardening parlance), which were taller versions of the same or different plants, were used to break the height and

Bright red geraniums shine like jewels set in the silver surround of grey foliage plants.

such as a stone statue or birdbath, has much the same effect, acting as a focal point and contrasting with the uniformity of the bedding plants.

EDGING

Edging is formal, repetitive planting, rather like bedding, but long and thin in plan, and low in elevation. Edging can 'frame' a formal bed or follow the straight or meandering lines of a mixed border or path.

Traditional edgings for geranium beds include ageratum, lobelia and sweet alyssum. For an attractive and patriotic combination, try planting red geraniums edged in alternating blue lobelia and white alyssum. Non-flowering golden feverfew or *Senecio cineraria* are foliage options, as is coleus, or flame nettle, almost as popular with the Victorians as geraniums themselves. Herbaceous perennial edging plants, such as sempervivum, catmint, pinks, erigeron or heuchera, or even shrubs such as clipped dwarf box or cotton lavender, save time and money.

Dwarf or miniature zonal geraniums, such as the old 'Black Vesuvius' or the new 'China Doll', with dark green leaves and salmon blooms, are ideal edging for beds of summer annuals. The non-flowering, bushy, silver-edged zonal 'Mme Salleron' makes a good edger, as does the bushy, ivy-leaved 'Sugar Baby' with its candy-pink

potential boredom. You can plant a single standard geranium, rose, fuchsia or marguerite in the centre of a round or small rectangular bed, or space several, at regular intervals, in a large rectangular or square one. A permanent plant, such as a topiary trained yew or box, or 'non-plant' feature,

blossoms. Either would be perfect in a Victorian-style garden, in keeping with the Victorian practice of edging green-leaved scarlet geraniums with ivy-leaved or variegated ones. More complicated edging, or 'ribbon bedding', in the Victorian style might include a row of blue lobelia, backed by a row of white-leaved *Senecio cineraria*, backed by a row of scarlet geraniums, backed by a row of yellow calceolaria, followed by a tall back row of dark-leaved *Perilla frutescens*.

When using geraniums for edging, plant miniatures and dwarfs 15–20cm (6–8in) apart, others 30cm (12in) apart.

GERANIUMS AS GROUND COVER
Geraniums are ideal as ground cover for areas where you wish to have a more casual, permanent outdoor bed, without the responsibility and high maintenance of formal beds. Naturally short-jointed, well-branched geranium cultivars like the bright red, semi-double Tavira are best. Alternatively, ivy-leaved geraniums, which are rarely used as the main subject of formal bedding, can make excellent ground cover for sunny banks or flat areas, especially in frost-free climates. As with bedding, the ground should be well weeded before the geraniums are planted. To encourage side shoots to form, the growing tips should be pinched out on a regular basis.

Formal rose beds often have bare soil; underplanting with a ground cover of ivy-leaved geraniums in toning or contrasting colours improves the overall appearance, and their wide-spreading, non-climbing habit is ideal for the job. Again, pinch out the growing tips frequently.

Geraniums intermingled with begonias, busy Lizzies and spider plants give added colour and romance to this ruined castle wall.

GERANIUMS IN THE HERB GARDEN

Scented-leaved geraniums are ideal for a sunny herb garden, where their modest appearance, subtle leaf variation and small flowers are an asset, not a handicap. They are also an appropriate selection, since many are used in cooking to scent foods (see pages 60–71) and oil of geranium can be distilled from *P. graveolens* and *P. capitatum* and used in making potpourri, perfumes and soaps. Dainty species and cultivars, such as *P. odoratissimum* or 'Attar of Roses', make good edging, while taller, more robust types, such as *P. graveolens* or 'Clorinda', can be used as focal points.

Scented-leaved geraniums provide not only a rich range of fragrances, but also a variety of leaf shapes, sizes and textures, from velvety and smooth to crisp and wrinkled. Public gardens sometimes feature these plants in raised beds to make their appreciation easier for the blind and for those in wheelchairs.

GERANIUMS IN ROCK GARDENS

Although true alpine enthusiasts would certainly disagree, there is a place for geraniums in the rock garden. Most popular rockery plants, such as aubrieta and alyssum, are spring- or early summer-flowering and rock gardens can look dull in summer. Dwarf and miniature geraniums have the right scale, if not provenance, for rock gardens, and a few tucked here and there can provide bright splashes of colour. Ivy-leaved geraniums, with their trailing habit, could be planted at the top of a rockery to cascade down.

GERANIUMS IN INFORMAL BEDDING

Bedding can be informal as well as formal, and informal groups of geraniums can be used as infill in mixed beds and borders. Planted in irregularly shaped groups of odd numbers, they can follow on after spring biennials, such as Sweet Williams, Canterbury bells, forget-me-nots or wallflowers have finished their display. Their sun-loving nature makes geraniums perfect partners for silver- and grey-leaved plants, such as cotton lavender, lavender, rosemary, shrubby helichrysum and senecio.

The naturally lax habit of ivy-leaved geraniums and some scented-leaved forms such as *P. tomentosum*, is, as we have seen, used to advantage in hanging baskets and urns, but they can also be grown in the open ground to trail over or cascade down sunny retaining walls or raised beds. You can grow spreading types in pockets of soil in gravel, where they benefit from the latter's perfect drainage and heat-reflective qualities, and will release their fragrance when brushed against by passers by.

GERANIUMS UNDER GLASS

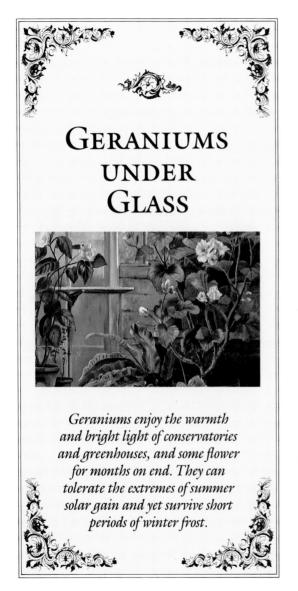

Geraniums enjoy the warmth and bright light of conservatories and greenhouses, and some flower for months on end. They can tolerate the extremes of summer solar gain and yet survive short periods of winter frost.

Conservatories and garden rooms are for the display of plants in their prime, and for the enjoyment of those who grow them. Many conservatories are annexed to the house to make additional living space, the dividing line between the two being deliberately blurred. Although some conservatories are jungle like and do require much work, most are a comfortable compromise between living, dining and play room, with a few plants thrown in. Popular types of geranium are easy going and decorative, and since bright sunlight is their main requirement, they are among the most reliable and popular conservatory plants.

The difference between greenhouse and conservatory is one of degree and attitude: a greenhouse is often separate from the house, treated as a functional space for the propagation, growth and overwintering of tender plants as well as possible display, and kept at a lower temperature than a conservatory used as a habitable room. Sunny, glassed-in front porches are variations on the theme; though often unheated, they usually provide enough protection for overwintering, provided the potting compost is kept bone dry.

All geraniums are suitable for greenhouse

Growing geraniums in a greenhouse or conservatory means that you can enjoy their flowers all year round.

or conservatory growing, with their high light needs and ability to thrive and flower well in small pots. In particular, those with large, fragile blooms, such as the regals, or tightly double trusses, such as the rosebud, or noisette, zonals, perform better under glass than in the open ground, since their blooms are protected from weather. For sheer length of display and plentiful colour, zonals are as reliable under glass as they are in the garden.

Decoratively, geraniums are as long as the proverbial piece of string. In conservatories where plants assume a minor role, zonal and zonal derivatives, singly or grouped in a large terra-cotta half pan, are perfect 'token' plants for a side table or shelf. Because of their inbred uniformity, they are excellent for massing: the indoor equivalent of bedding-out schemes. With several pots grouped in a larger cache pot, a nice finishing touch, is to hide the rims of the individual pots with a layer of moss. In conservatories with solid lower walls, you can rest geranium-filled window boxes on the sills, perhaps mirroring similar window boxes outside.

Victorian-style tiered wirework plant stands can hold as many pots of geraniums

Create an Edwardian idyll in your conservatory with pink geraniums – a perfect setting for tea on a sunny afternoon.

as the space allows, creating an overall effect of height, although the individual plants are compact. Such stands (and old-fashioned, slatted, greenhouse staging), being perforated, have another advantage: they allow air to circulate freely around the plants and help prevent the stagnant, still conditions that geraniums so dislike. Small pots of geraniums can add low-level interest, clustered round the base of large foliage plants, such as jasmine, but make sure the geraniums have sufficient light and are not liable to be trodden on or knocked over.

You can take a 'designer approach', confining your choice to a single flower colour, or, say, shades of pink, to tone in with your decor. Or you can take a pure collector's approach, with single specimens of as many different species, varieties and cultivars as there is space for, displayed in well-labelled, straightforward rows, with no attempt at aesthetic integration. You can create a colourful indoor flower garden, with much the same mix of summery plants – geraniums, fuchsias, petunias, ageratum, begonias – as in the garden outdoors. Or you can try a more sophisticated approach, with geraniums providing occasional colour against a largely foliar, jungle-like setting, possibly using scented-leaved geraniums as part of the foliage. Lastly, the species can be placed in a natural-looking setting, with pots buried in sandy, rocky grit simulating the

Above: *Add fragrance as well as colour to your conservatory or greenhouse by training scented geraniums against a solid wall.*

Right: *This bedding-out scheme under glass features an edging of variegated-leaved zonal geraniums, with mixed zonals behind, and scented-leaved geraniums as 'dot plants'.*

plants' native environment, as is often done in botanical gardens.

Because geraniums need a dry atmosphere they are unsuitable for combining with tropical plants, such as white sails, *Spathiphyllum*, or the stag's-horn fern, *Platycerium bifurcatum*, which need constant high humidity, although tough ferns, such as the holly-leaf fern, *Cyrtomium falcatum*, can be grown in the shade under staging or plant display stands.

In a conservatory decorated and used as additional living space, you can place clay or plastic pots of geraniums into more decorative outer containers, such as bamboo, wicker or glazed ceramic cache pots, or urns on raised pedestals, to match the decor. Watering must, however, be very carefully controlled, since excess water remains in the outer pot, and can rot the roots.

If you have open beds against the solid house wall of a conservatory, you can grow zonal, ivy-leaved or strong-growing scented-leaved geraniums to reach jungle-like proportions. Place a 15cm (6in) layer of drainage material, such as broken clay flower pots, in the bottom, and cover it with fine mesh before adding the potting compost, to prevent the compost filtering through and blocking the drainage. Space plants 60–90cm (2–3ft) apart, and tie in new growth to canes, wires or trellis. Pinch out growing tips, as necessary, to encourage

This 19th-century painting shows cold frames, with the glass covers removed, where geraniums were traditionally placed in high summer, when the greenhouse received its annual clean.

side shoots to form. Prune only when the allotted space is used up, by removing older stems and tying in young replacement ones to fill the space.

Uniques, with their naturally strong, erect habit, are especially suitable for open

This doll's house, with its bower of ivy-leaved geraniums, would be an enchanting focal point in any conservatory.

strong growth, are also very good for open borders. Whatever type you use, you can interplant with climbers needing similar conditions: the South African Cape leadwort, *Plumbago capensis*, for example.

Ivy-leaved types can be trained from ground level up a wall and along the greenhouse or conservatory ridge, using wires, for a bower-like effect. Pinch out frequently, to prevent them becoming lank and leggy. Alternatively, place pots of ivy-leaved geraniums on a tall shelf and allow the stems to trail, forming a waterfall effect of foliage and flowers. Placing the pot on another, upturned pot gives a little additional height, if needed. Hanging baskets filled with three or four of the same variety of ivy-leaved geraniums are traditional, hung centrally, along the ridge, or from brackets attached to walls or columns. Pots of ivy-leaved geraniums can also be rested in wall-hung wire pot holders. The naturally sprawling, scented-leaved *P. tomentosum* is also good for large hanging baskets, mixed with zonals and ivy-leaved types, adding perfume as well as a soft, grey foliage backdrop for the flowers of other types.

Naturally tall, strong-growing scented-leaved types, such as *P. graveolens* or its variegated form, can be grown in large pots to create tall columns of greenery. A row of such plants, placed close together, becomes a solid wall of greenery and, as a bonus,

borders, provided you pinch out the growing tips regularly. They tend to be bare at the base, and lower-growing geraniums, such as the miniature or dwarf zonals, could be grown in front, to conceal their legginess. The American Irene strains, with their naturally self-branching habit and

provides sprigs of cut foliage for flower arranging all year round. Or you can place a pair of large pots of columnar, scented-leaved geraniums either side of the door joining the conservatory to the house, to release their fragrance as the leaves are touched in passing. Strong-growing scented-leaved and zonal geraniums can also be trained as standards, displayed either side of the greenhouse or conservatory door.

In small greenhouses or conservatories, where space is limited, you can grow naturally small geraniums, such as the Miniatures, Dwarfs, or compact F_1 hybrids; or, with stronger growing types, you could institute a program of annual renewal – extra work but resulting in a continual stock of young, healthy, non-woody, floriferous small plants.

Whether you move pot-grown greenhouse and conservatory geraniums outdoors during the summer is a matter of choice. Shading and watering are easier outdoors, and insect pests, such as whitefly, tend to be less troublesome outdoors. For some people, the whole point of overwintering geraniums is to use them in the summer garden with the greenhouse as simply storage space. On the other hand, you may not have a suitably sunny spot, or you may just prefer to enjoy an indoor garden in addition to, or as a substitute for, an outdoor one.

Above: *The geraniums ranged along this wall reflect those inside the conservatory and help soften the division between the inside and outside of the house.*

Right: *This carnival of colours combines zonal, regal and cactus-flowered geraniums for a tropical, Mardi-Gras effect.*

CUT AND DRIED FLOWERCRAFT

Today, geraniums are used almost exclusively as pot or garden plants and rarely appear in flower-arranging books. The Victorians, however, recognized their value as cut flowers, with their bright colours and long-lasting qualities

In Victorian times, cut geraniums were often partnered with garden or greenhouse flowers and foliage, such as fuchsia, ivy, moss and fern, in elaborately ornate displays. While ornateness is unlikely to return to popularity, the use of geraniums as cut flowers could well do!

Unless you are also pruning the plant when cutting flowers, the relatively short flower stalk limits the use of geraniums to small arrangements, or the base of larger ones, but there is still scope for creativity, and modest displays are often the most charming. If you can space the flowering time, by nipping out the flower buds in summer, and providing adequate light and warmth, you can induce zonal types to flower in late autumn and winter, when a free source of cut flowers is very welcome.

SUITABLE TYPES OF FLOWERS AND FOLIAGE

Nothing takes the place of experimenting; by testing cut flowers of particular geranium cultivars before you actually need them, you can avoid last-minute disappointments. Zonal, regal and variations of the two – nosegay, Deacon, Uniques, Irenes, Angels, dwarf and miniatures – generally last up to two weeks in water. Deacon types are especially good for holding their petals.

The value of cut geranium foliage is also underestimated. While the beauty of regals

The French flower painter Henri Fantin-Latour perfectly captures the beauty of cut geraniums in a simple glass vase.

the base, to hide florist's foam blocks or other foundations.

Strong-growing scented-leaved types, such as *P. graveolens* or *P. filicifolium*, can provide long branches, and the plants benefit from the pruning. Especially enchanting are the slightly sinuous stems of the little *P. crispum* 'Variegatum', which add interesting outlines and contrast to bulky blooms, such as double peonies and roses. The graceful trailing stems of ivy-leaved types are invaluable for softening the hard line between plant material and container.

CONDITIONING AND CARE

Pick the flowers in bud or with just a few flowers open, since the buds open in water and fully open flowers are extremely fragile and liable to shatter. Snap (don't tear) or cut the stalk cleanly where it joins the main stem. Immerse immediately in water up to the neck and leave for several hours.

To condition foliage, strip all leaves that will be submerged in the display. If the stem is woody and hard, scrape the lowest 2.5cm (12in) of bark, but don't crush it, as this makes it difficult to insert the stem in florist's foam and encourages rotting.

A drop of bleach in the vase water extends the life of the cut material. If you use florist's foam make a pilot hole first with a wire or toothpick to avoid damaging soft stalks or stems. Keep the display away from

and plain-leaved zonals lies mainly in their flowers, many scented-leaved types have foliage as attractive as any florist's fern, and the tricolour and golden-leaved zonals provide material for miniature arrangements. Single zonal leaves are ideal for tucking into

direct sunlight, draughts and radiators. Top up with fresh water as necessary. Regular mist spraying in hot weather or centrally heated rooms is also helpful, as is removing faded leaves and fallen petals.

SEASONAL ARRANGEMENTS

With the abundance of flowers available in summer, few think of using cut geraniums. However, they partner roses beautifully, and their unusual colour juxtapositions can be marvellously arresting. You can fill a raised, shallow bowl or upturned straw hat with semi-double or double zonal blooms, each dense head surrounded by a ruffle of its own leaves. Packed tightly in this way, the flowers are especially long lasting, with the petals held in place by compaction.

The lower, flowering side shoots of delphiniums are a similar length to geranium stalks, and pale pink zonals and pale blue delphinium florets are a charming, old-fashioned combination. For a stronger colour scheme, use the acid green flowers of lady's mantle or rich blue cornflowers with scarlet geraniums.

Summer is also the season of abundant foliage, and cool, all-foliage displays make a pleasant change from colourful flowers. Combine stems of scented-leaved geraniums, such as *P. crispum* 'Variegatum', or golden-leaved zonals with any combination of the following: the trailing, silvery *Ballota pseudodictamnus*; asparagus fern; hosta; rue; variegated ivy or *Sedum sieboldii* 'Variegata'. Poetic licence allows the inclusion of green flowers and seed pods, such as the flowering tobacco, *Nicotiana* 'Lime Green'; *Zinnia* 'Envy'; the greeny yellow *Iris foetidissima*; *Heuchera* 'Greenfinch'; *Rosa chinensis* 'Viridis'; lady's mantle and green honesty seed pods. For an unusual focal point, use succulent, flower-like echeveria rosettes.

Bowls of freshly picked, scented-leaved geranium leaves, mixed with lemon verbena leaves, sprigs of rosemary and other aromatic foliage, are lovely finishing touches to a summer lunch or dinner party indoors. Try to pick them at the last minute.

Autumn colours in the garden suit scarlet, cerise and magenta geraniums, which invite riotous displays with similarly coloured dahlias, zinnias and love-lies-bleeding, clashing in the nicest possible way. Combining these red-hot tones with purple-leaved Venetian sumach, or smoke bush, or with purple-leaved sage, or the pinkish grey foliage of *Rosa rubrifolia* is very effective. Even a few russety autumnal bracken fronds can transform one or two geranium flowers into an arrangement. For stunning contrast, combine bright pink, intense red or scarlet

Scarlet, crimson and purple geraniums are ideal for combining with autumn fruits, berries and foliage for an intensely rich-looking display.

zonals with the equally intense blue of autumn gentians or the hardy plumbago, *Ceratostigma willmottianum*.

Autumn is also the season for ornamental berries, and geraniums can be partnered with rose hips, pyracantha, fishbone cotoneaster or short, leafless branches of crab-apple. Rich purple regals and bluey-back elderberries are super together, but elderberry juice stains, so beware of stray berries on carpets or upholstery! Wired clusters of black grapes are a safer alternative.

In winter, the red and white of zonals are ideal for Christmas arrangements, with sprigs of holly or, more subtly, mistletoe in berry. Evergreen foliage, such as yew, euonymus, elaeagnus, spruce or laurustinus is also festive, with white variegated leaves that are especially nice with white geraniums. A pedestal vase with white geraniums and trails of white-variegated periwinkle is elegant, festive and unusual. For Christmas decorations with an oriental flair, combine red or white zonal blooms with wired-up pine cones, contorted willow, or bare larch or alder branches with their decorative cones.

If you have enough flowers, fill a low, shallow dish with densely packed red geraniums, inserting a few silver, gold or red Christmas tree balls among them. White spider chrysanthemums are a staple Christmas florist's flower, and combine well with white or red geranium blossom. For a small display, buy one stem of spider 'mum'; cut the side flowers off individually, and use the upper cluster of flowers as a single stem. White geraniums, white spray carnations, gypsophila and short stems of white-variegated ivy-leaved geranium foliage work well together in various combinations.

Spring brings the possibility of mixed pinks: geraniums, tulip, crab-apple blossom, hyacinths, polyanthus and bergenia; of mauve regals and lilac; and of scented-leaved geranium foliage, green hellebore buds and unripe seed pods. In a wide, shallow dish you could create a short-stemmed 'forest' of zonal geranium flowers stuck upright on a bed of moss.

For a late spring display, combine pink zonal geraniums, lily-of-the-valley, grape hyacinths, forget-me-nots, snake's head fritillaries, and lungwort, ivy, variegated tradescantia and bugle foliage. On a simple note, use a ruff of variegated geranium leaves around a tight bunch of primrose or violets, and place it in a wine glass or other small receptacle.

Most geranium flowers are long-lasting when cut and will augment any arrangement beautifully. Here they share the foreground with some pinks in a tall arrangement of English summer flowers.

POT ET FLEUR ARRANGEMENTS

Except for some scented-leaved types, geraniums have unmemorable growth habits and, when out of flower, zonals and regals in particular can lose their appeal. Placing several foliage plants together in a communal display with cut flowers – 'pot et fleur' – is a traditional practice of flower arranging, for which scented-leaved and out-of-flower geranium plants are prime candidates. The resulting display has more visual impact –ideal for a dinner party or other social occasion – than the sum of its parts. Some crowding is necessary to get a generous effect and geraniums need freely circulating air, so treat the the display as temporary. It can, however, remain intact for several weeks before dismantling, and fresh flowers can replace wilted ones.

Large, deep containers, such as wicker baskets lined with polythene, or stoneware or enamelled casseroles, can hold several plants. You can leave them in their pots, or decant them; either way, place a layer of pebbles or broken flower pots in the bottom for drainage, and fill the spaces between the pots or rootballs with damp peat.

Decide whether the display is to be viewed from every direction or the front only, and arrange plants accordingly. You can camouflage leggy geraniums by tilting some plants slightly forwards or including other, low-growing house plants, such as ivy or spider plant, but avoid those, such as ferns, that need more water than geraniums. Place a small jar, filled with water or saturated florist's foam, centrally or to one side to hold the cut flowers. Insert the flowers, then cover the surface with sphagnum or bun moss, or water-washed pebbles.

Some flowers, such as dahlias, chrysanthemums, lilacs and alstroemeria, have crude, small or quick-wilting foliage, often removed during conditioning. These are ideal to display in a big basket of geraniums, but you can also use dried or good-quality silk flowers, especially since fabric foliage is generally inferior to fabric flowers, and dried flowers have no foliage attached. Because you don't have to confine dried or silk flowers to a water receptacle, you could create a fantastic arrangement, with a 'forest' of fantasy flowers among the plants.

SCENTED-LEAVED GERANIUM POTPOURRIS

Potpourris are like salads – the ingredients and proportions are a matter of personal taste and availability. The following recipes are good basic starters, but you can adjust

---

A charming example of a 'pot et fleur' arrangement – the green and white motif using dwarf chrysanthemums and geraniums with cut phlox and anemones has a crisp, summery look.

them as you like. The only proviso is to go easy on the amount of essential oils used; too much can give the potpourri a crude, 'dime store' odour.

Method

In all cases, the instructions are the same. Mix the ingredients thoroughly, adding the oil drop by drop. Place in an airtight container in a dark, warm place for at least a month, shaking daily. Transfer to potpourri pots or ornamental bowls.

ROSE GERANIUM POTPOURRI

Rose and lavender are the two prime floral ingredients of traditional potpourri, since they are widely available and their fragrance is long lasting. In this recipe, rose geranium leaves and oil add to the general 'rosiness'.

½cup dried rose geranium leaves

— · —

½cup dried lavender blossom

— · —

½cup dried mint leaves

— · —

½cup dried rose petals

— · —

7.5ml (1½tsp) orris root powder

— · —

1 crushed cinnamon stick

— · —

6 crushed cloves

— · —

3 drops rose geranium oil

RAINBOW POTPOURRI

Some potpourris can look dusty, but this recipe is as colourful as it is fragrant. If you do dried flower arranging, it's an excellent recipe for using dried flowers that have broken off their stems.

½cup dried pink rose petals

— · —

½cup dried red rose petals

— · —

½cup dried yellow rose petals

— · —

½cup dried lavender blossom

— · —

½cup dried blue delphinium petals

— · —

½cup dried blue cornflowers

— · —

½cup dried yellow pot marigold petals

— · —

½cup dried orange pot marigold petals

— · —

½cup dried rose-scented geranium leaves

— · —

½cup dried lemon verbena leaves

— · —

22.5ml (1½Tbs) dried orris root powder

— · —

7.5ml (½tsp) freshly ground nutmeg

— · —

7.5ml (½tsp) freshly ground cloves

— · —

7.5ml (½tsp) ground cinnamon

— · —

9 drops rose geranium oil

LEMON GERANIUM POTPOURRI

This unusual, yellow and green potpourri is strongly scented of lemon, from a variety of sources.

1 cup dried lemon geranium leaves

— · —

½cup dried lemon verbena leaves

— · —

½cup dried lemon balm leaves

— · —

1 cup dried chamomile flowers

— · —

½cup dried yellow pot marigold petals

— · —

½cup dried yellow African marigold petals

— · —

15ml (1Tbs) orris root powder

— · —

6 drops lemon geranium oil

— · —

1 dried lemon peel, cut into small strips

— · —

PRESSING PETALS AND LEAVES

Pressing geranium flowers and foliage for dried flowercrafts is Victorian in origin. Today, you can use a flower press or, as then, insert the flowers between pieces of tissue paper in the pages of a heavy book.

Choose dry, blemish-free flowers and foliage; intricate, scented-leaved foliage is especially valuable, and can be substituted for ferns in pressed flower landscapes. Thick, succulent or woolly leaves are harder to press successfully than thin ones. Single flowers are easier to press than double ones; remember that red flowers darken considerably. Split the flower heads apart into individual florets for pressing; you can, if wished, reassemble them when dry. The beak-like seed heads can also be dried.

Once pressed, you can use the material in dried flower pictures, cards or other decorative crafts. For those keen on Victoriana, the nineteenth-century 'language of flowers' assigned specific meanings to popular garden and wild flowers, and secret messages were sent between lovers via bouquets and floral cards. Nutmeg geranium meant an expected meeting; oak-leaved geranium, true friendship; scarlet geranium, comfort; rose-scented geranium, preference; lemon geranium, unexpected meeting; and dark red geranium, melancholy.

HERB PILLOWS

These small, fragrant cushions are for placing under your pillow at night. Scenting a bed in this way can be traced back to the Roman practice of stuffing mattresses with fragrant grasses and herbs; the British wildflower, *Galium verum*, derives its common name, lady's bedstraw, from that use. If wished, you can use cotton wadding to bulk out the mixture. Sprigged, Liberty-style floral fine cotton or silk make nice covers; lace and ribbon trim are optional extras.

LEMON AND LAVENDER HERB PILLOW

1 cup lemon-scented geranium leaves

— · —

½cup lemon thyme leaves

— · —

½cup lemon verbena leaves

— · —

1 cup lavender blossom

— · —

15ml (1Tbs) powdered orris root

— · —

5ml (1tsp) freshly grated nutmeg

Crush the dried herbs, then mix with the orris root and nutmeg. Place in a sealed, airtight jar and leave in a dark place, stirring occasionally, for at least four weeks. When sewing the pillow up, leave one corner loosely stitched, so that when the fragrance fades you can open the pillow and add a drop or two of essential oil.

PUNGENT HERB PILLOW

1 cup dried lemon-scented geranium leaves

— · —

½cup dried rosemary leaves

— · —

½cup dried lemon verbena leaves

— · —

1 cup dried pine needles

— · —

15ml (1Tbs) orris root powder

Crush the dried leaves, then mix with the orris root. Place in a sealed, airtight jar and proceed as in the recipe above.

COOKERY AND COSMETIC USE

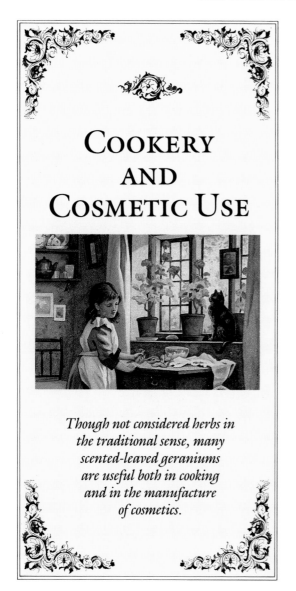

Though not considered herbs in the traditional sense, many scented-leaved geraniums are useful both in cooking and in the manufacture of cosmetics.

Scented-leaved geraniums can add fragrance to a range of dishes, savoury as well as sweet. As with most herbs and spices, it is safer to use too little than too much – you will be surprised how intense the fragrance can be from even a single leaf. Always thoroughly wash and dry the leaves before use. It is best to avoid using leaves that have come in contact with insecticides and fungicides, but if this is not possible, always follow the manufacturers' warnings concerning the minimum time lapse between applying the chemical and harvesting. If in doubt, as with a newly bought plant for example, allow the maximum time to lapse before using.

Interestingly, geraniums are rich in vitamin C, but the taste and fragrance of a particular scented-leaf form often differ. Many scented-leaved types taste acidic and grassy, and some are extremely acrid. A few have a pleasing, refreshing, pepperminty flavour, and can be chopped up and incorporated into recipes. Others should be used during cooking to add fragrance and then removed before serving. For the passionate devotee to the genus, the bright green leaves of zonal cultivars, which can be cooked and served like spinach, have a taste somewhat like asparagus or cabbage.

The following list is just a rough guideline. A variety that to one nose smells of nutmeg, to another might smell of eucalyptus, camphor, turpentine or pine; different scents are attributed to the same species in different catalogues. Some varieties have a mixture of scents, such as lemony or minty rose. Always smell a scented-leaved geranium before using it in a recipe to make sure that its particular scent matches your expectations. As you become a 'connoisseur', you will be able to distinguish between one variety of lemon-scented geranium and another, and have added impetus for increasing your collection.

SCENTED-LEAVED GERANIUMS

ROSE SCENT

P. 'Attar of Roses'

P. capitatum

P. graveolens
(mint flavoured)

'Grey Lady Plymouth'

'Lady Plymouth'

'Lady Scarborough'

'Little Gem'

'Queen of Roses'

P. radens

'Rober's Lemon Rose'

GINGER SCENT

'Toronto'

LEMON SCENT

P. crispum major

P. crispum minor

P. crispum 'Variegatum'

'Lemon Fancy'

'Mabel Grey' (mint flavoured)

'Pink Champagne'

LIME SCENT

P. × nervosum

APPLE SCENT

P. odoratissimum

ORANGE SCENT

P. 'American Prince of Orange'

P. 'Prince of Orange'

SPICY SCENT

P. fragile

P. × fragrans

P. × fragrans 'Variegatum'
('Creamy Nutmeg',
'Snowy Nutmeg')

'Lady Mary'

P. trifolium

COCONUT SCENT

P. grossularioides

MINT SCENT

'Joy Lucille'

P. tomentosum*
(mint flavoured)

LEMON GERANIUM CAKE

Popular cultivars with lemon-scented foliage include 'Mabel Grey', with huge, palmate leaves, and P. crispum major and minor, with tiny, crinkled leaves. You need only two leaves of 'Mabel Grey' for this recipe, but eight of P. crispum minor – use common sense to adjust numbers, in this and the following recipes.

2 large, 4 medium-sized or 8 small lemon-scented geranium leaves, washed and dried

— · —

150g/5oz self-raising flour, plus extra for flouring

— · —

30ml/2Tbs milk

— · —

5ml/1tsp baking powder

— · —

pinch of salt

— · —

2 large eggs

— · —

125g/4oz softened butter, plus extra for greasing

— · —

125g/4oz caster sugar

— · —

5ml/1tsp grated lemon rind

— · —

4 crystallized scented geranium leaves

For the icing
150g/5 oz softened, unsalted butter

— · —

300g/10oz icing sugar, sifted

— · —

5ml/1tsp grated lemon rind

— · —

5ml/1tsp lemon juice

1 Slightly bruise the leaves by rubbing them against the inside of a medium-sized bowl. Sift the flour into the bowl, stir in the leaves and cover with clingfilm. Leave for at least an hour, stirring occasionally.

2 Meanwhile, preheat the oven to 180°C/350°F/gas mark 4. Grease and flour two 20cm/8in sandwich tins. Remove the leaves from the flour, flatten them out and divide between the 2 tins.

3 Add the remaining cake ingredients to the flour and beat or blend until smooth. Divide between the 2 tins and bake for 20–25 minutes, or until the cake starts to come away from the sides of the tin. Half-way through, swap them round on the shelves, to ensure even baking. Cool, then turn out and carefully remove the leaves.

4 Meanwhile, make the icing. Cream the butter, slowly add the sugar, then the grated lemon rind and juice. Use one third to sandwich the cakes together, and the rest to ice the top and sides. Before serving, decorate with the crystallized scented geranium leaves (see page 64).

Serves 6–8

* All cup measurements are US cups or 8 oz.

CRYSTALLIZED GERANIUM LEAVES

Use crystallized scented geranium leaves with crystallized rose petals, violets or primroses to create a summery garland on a cake, whatever the time of year, or use the leaves on their own. Leaves range from palmate, lobed and arrow shaped to round, and from solid to lacy, but make sure the scent is suitable for a dessert.

scented geranium leaves, washed and dried

— . —

egg white

— . —

caster sugar

1 Gently break up the egg white with a fork. Pour the sugar into a shallow bowl. Using a small, soft artist's brush, coat both sides of a leaf with the egg white. Dip in the sugar, thoroughly coating both sides. Brush with egg white and dip in sugar again, then place on a wire rack. Repeat until all the leaves are coated.

2 Place the rack in the bottom of a very low oven with the door left ajar, for 10–15 minutes, or until dry and crispy. Cool, then store in an airtight container.

HERB GERANIUM BUTTER

When rolled and sliced into rounds, this butter makes a flavourful garnish to steaks, chops, fish, baked potatoes and hot vegetable dishes. The finer you chop the geranium leaves, the better. Chives are more easily dealt with using scissors; thyme leaves, being naturally diminutive, simply need stripping from their wiry stems.

5ml/1tsp freshly snipped chives

— . —

5ml/1tsp freshly chopped parsley

— . —

5ml/1tsp fresh thyme

— . —

2.5ml/½tsp freshly chopped lemon-scented geranium leaves

— . —

175g/6oz salted butter, slightly softened

1 Work the herbs into the butter, mixing until they are evenly distributed. Chill for a few minutes.

2 Turn onto aluminium foil and pat into shape, forming the butter into a long roll, about 4cm/1½in wide. Wrap and chill.

3 Before serving, cut into slices 6–8mm/ ¼–⅓in thick.

LIME POTTED PRAWNS

If you can't get the admittedly rare P. nervosum, *use a lemon-scented type. Brown bread and butter are the traditional accompaniments to this first course or light luncheon dish.*

6 medium-sized, lime-scented geranium leaves

— · —

175g(6oz) butter

— · —

225g(8oz) peeled, fresh or defrosted frozen prawns, plus extra for garnishing

— · —

2.5ml/½ tsp mace

— · —

2.5ml/½ tsp cayenne pepper

— · —

2.5ml/½ tsp crushed green peppercorns

— · —

pinch of salt

1 Crush 2 leaves with your fingers and place the leaves and butter in a small saucepan over a low heat. When the butter is frothing but before its starts to brown, remove from the heat, skim and leave for 30 minutes for the mixture to steep.

2 Remove the leaves, add the prawns and seasoning and cook over a low heat, stirring for 3–4 minutes, until the prawns are cooked, if fresh, and the mixture is very hot but not colouring.

3 Spoon into 4 ramekins, pressing the shrimps lightly, to make sure they are covered by the butter. Cool, then chill.

4 Before serving, garnish each with a few prawns and a geranium leaf.

Serves 4

SWEET 'N' TANGY BARBECUE SAUCE

Give chicken, chops, steaks or spare ribs an extra lift with this subtle barbecue sauce.

2 garlic cloves

— · —

4 medium-sized lemon-scented geranium leaves

— · —

125ml/4fl oz/½ cup* runny honey

— · —

125ml/4fl oz/½ cup dark soy sauce

— · —

125ml/4fl oz/½ cup olive oil

— · —

15ml/1Tbs vinegar

— · —

2.5ml/½ tsp ground ginger

— · —

pinch of salt

Crush the garlic and finely chop the scented geranium leaves. Mix all the ingredients and use as a marinade or for basting.

* All cup measurements are US cups or 8 oz.

THICK GERANIUM
BLACKBERRY JELLY

You can make as much jelly as you like, but less than 450g/1lb of blackberries is rather fiddly for the amount of washing up involved, and over 2.2kg/5lb at a time is unwieldy.

blackberries

— . —

preserving sugar

— . —

scented geranium leaves, roughly 1 medium-sized
leaf per 450g/1lb blackberries

1 Wash and pick over the blackberries and stew with geranium leaves, a medium-sized leaf per every approximate pound, in a little water over low heat until soft. Sieve to remove the pips and leaves, and return the pulp to the pot. For each 550ml/ 20fl oz/2½cups* pulp, add 450g/1lb sugar.

2 Heat slowly to dissolve the sugar, then bring to a rapid boil, stirring, until the mixture jells, about 15 minutes. Check by dropping a small amount on a cold plate. Leave for a few minutes, then push it gently with your finger or a spoon. If it has started to solidify and form a wrinkled surface, it is ready.

3 Draw off the heat and skim. Pour or ladle into clean, dry, warm jars, cover with waxed paper discs and seal.

ROSE GERANIUM
ICE CREAM

Cultivars with rose-scented foliage include 'Attar of Roses', with prolific mauve flowers and a hint of lemon to its flowery scent: 'Lady Scarborough', with purple veined, pink flowers; and 'Grey Lady Plymouth', with silvery foliage and purple-veined rose blossom.

6–8 medium-sized rose geranium leaves, washed
and dried

— . —

700ml/25 fl oz/3 cups* double cream

— . —

6 egg yolks

— . —

300g/10oz caster sugar

— . —

pinch of salt

— . —

2–3 drops red food colouring (optional)

— . —

rose petals and geranium leaves, to decorate
(optional)

1 Place the leaves and cream in a saucepan. Heat to just below boiling point, then set aside, off the heat, to infuse for 30 minutes.

2 Place the egg yolks, sugar and salt in a bowl and whisk until the mixture is pale and leaves a trail when the whisk is lifted.

3 Strain the cream slowly into the egg mixture, whisking as you pour. Add 2–3 drops red food colouring, if wished.

* All cup measurements are US cups or 8 oz.

4 Return the mixture to the saucepan and cook over very low heat, stirring constantly, until the mixture is thick enough to coat the back of a wooden spoon. Cool, stirring from time to time.

5 Pour the mixture into a plastic freezer container, then freeze until hard to a depth of 2.5cm/1in round the edges.

6 Turn into a chilled bowl, whisk until smooth, then quickly return to the freezer. Repeat at least once more.

7 Remove from the freezer 20 minutes before serving, to soften slightly. Transfer to serving bowls and decorate, if wished, with fresh rose petals and geranium leaves.

Serves 6–8

ROSE GERANIUM SUGAR

Use this to flavour fruit salads, cakes, icings and iced teas. It is sensible to prepare a 500g/1.1lb or 1kg/2.2lb bag of sugar at a time.

caster sugar
— · —
rose-scented geranium leaves, washed and dried

Place a 2.5cm/1in layer of sugar in an airtight storage jar. Gently bruise a few leaves, to release their fragrance, and place on top of the sugar. Repeat until all the sugar and leaves are used. Cover, label and leave for at least 24 hours before use.

GERANIUM ICED TEA

Float one or two fresh lemon-scented geranium leaves in this cool summer drink.
P. tomentosum is especially nice in herbal teas, hot or cold, but rose-scented leaves could be used instead.

4 teabags or 30ml (/2Tbs) loose tea
— · —
6 medium-sized lemon-scented geranium leaves, washed
— · —
12 cloves
— · —
thinly sliced lemon, to decorate
— · —
crushed ice, to decorate
— · —
sugar (optional)

1 Place the tea, geranium leaves and cloves in a warmed teapot. Fill with 600ml/20fl oz/2½ cups* boiling water, leave to infuse for 5 minutes, then strain, cool and chill.

2 Fill tumblers with crushed ice, then pour over the tea, and decorate each glass with a lemon slice. Sweeten, if wished.

Serves 4

* All cup measurements are US cups or 8 oz.

SCENTED GERANIUM FACE CREAM

250ml/8fl oz/1 cup* almond oil

— . —

50g/2oz/¼ cup lanolin

— . —

1 cup lemon- or rose-scented geranium leaves

1 Place the almond oil and lanolin in a saucepan and heat gently, stirring. Add the leaves, stir, and steep for 30 minutes, over very low heat.

2 Pressing down on the leaves, strain the mixture and pour into small, wide-mouthed jars.

GERANIUM BATH OIL

Use 15ml/1Tbs of this aromatic oil in bathwater, as a treat for your skin.

1 cup rose- or lemon-scented geranium leaves

— . —

300ml/10fl oz/1¼cups baby oil

— . —

2 drops oil of geranium

Place all the ingredients in a jar and leave to steep.

* All cup measurements are US cups or 8 oz.

ICED GERANIUM BOWL

For a really superb effect, make a transparent ice bowl embedded with geranium leaves and flowers, and filled with ice cream or fruit salad. Scented leaved species with small flowers and delicate leaves, such as *P. odoratissimum, P. crispum* or *P. filicifolium*, are best.

Use two bowls of similar shape but different sizes. Part fill the larger bowl with water, leaves and flowers, and then place the smaller bowl on top, weighting it down if necessary, so that the water comes up to the rim, but there is still sufficient depth between the two bowl bases to form a solid base. Alternatively, fill in a ring mould with water, flowers and foliage. Freeze until solid.

Just before serving, turn out, dipping the bowls or moulds very briefly in hot water first, if necessary. If you use a transparent glass outer bowl, you can just remove the inner one. Place the bowl right way up on a serving platter, and invert the ring mould. Fill the centre, decorate with more flowers and leaves, and serve.

LOOKING AFTER GERANIUMS

Most geranium species come from frost-free, desert or semi-desert regions in South Africa, with hot, brilliant sun and well-drained soil. The more closely you can recreate these natural conditions, the more success you will have in growing healthy plants.

Although the factors affecting the well-being of geraniums are set out separately below, a change in one, such as increased light, usually requires an adjustment in others, such as increased water. As you become experienced, you develop a natural rhythm, and can make these adjustments almost without thinking. Try to make changes gradually; do not, for example, go from watering monthly to watering daily, or move plants from centrally heated to near freezing conditions, in one step. 'Moderation in all things' applies to caring for geraniums, too.

LIGHT

Bright sunlight promotes strong, bushy but compact growth and good flowering; in poor light, growth is spindly and flowers are few. In frost-free, relatively dry areas, plants can stay outside all year round. In cooler, northern temperate climates, a south- or west-facing greenhouse, conservatory, or window sill is fine for overwintering or growing all year round, but clean the glass in autumn to ensure that maximum light reaches plants in winter.

Light needs vary slightly from type to type. Ivy-leaved geraniums, being suc-

This greenhouse windowsill is an ideal spot for geraniums in temperate climates, as it lets in plenty of light.

culent, need the most light, while regal types need shade from strong light under glass, especially when in bloom.

HEAT AND HUMIDITY

It is safest to treat all geraniums as frost tender. In fact, they vary in their tolerance of cold, according to type, but mature plants and those growing in dry conditions tolerate lower temperatures than those with soft growth or in damp soil or atmosphere. The winter ideal is 4°C(39°F), but miniatures, tricolor zonals and many scented-leaved types prefer a few degrees warmer. Sturdy, green zonal types tolerate a few degrees of frost, if the air and soil or compost are dry. While geraniums generally thrive in warmth, their roots prefer a lower temperature than their top growth, rather like clematis, and cool temperatures accelerate flowering in regals.

High humidity in cold weather causes fungal infections. This is not normally a problem in a house or conservatory used as a family room but in a greenhouse, increasing the heat and ventilation decreases the humidity. Even a cold fan switched on for a few hours a day helps increase air circulation, thus discouraging botrytis.

FEEDING AND WATERING

Newly potted plants have enough nutrients for six weeks in peat-based composts, and up to 12 weeks in loam-based ones. Generally, however, the more you water, the more you should feed. In winter, if you water weekly, feed every six weeks or so. In summer, you might water daily, so feed once a week. Liquid feeds or water-soluble powder feeds added to water are easiest to vary, but you can also use slow-release food spikes or tablets inserted into the compost, or fertilizer-impregnated mats placed under pots, from early spring until early autumn. Always follow manufacturers' instructions: too much feed can be fatal.

Ideally, geraniums need a high nitrate feed to start the growing season, for shoot and leaf growth, followed by a feed high in potassium, such as liquid tomato fertilizer, to encourage flowering. Some professional growers spray the foliage of green-leaved types with Epsom salts (magnesium sulphate) in the growing season, to improve leaf colour.

It is better to underwater than to overwater. Water sparingly when heat and light are low, allowing the compost to become almost bone dry between waterings – in an unheated room in winter, water once a week, a fortnight or even once a month. Try not to get water in the leaves, as this encourages botrytis. In spring and summer, when active growth occurs, water whenever the top of the compost looks and feels dry; dry compost is paler than wet, and the pot feels light when lifted. In hot weather, this could be daily. Remember that small pots dry out more quickly than large ones. Whatever the time of year, plants forming flower buds and in full bloom need a steady supply of water. If you use a greenhouse, consider capillary matting, from which water is absorbed as needed into the compost in the pots by capillary action.

If compost, especially peat-based, dries out, stand the pot in a bucket or sink full of water, until air bubbles stop rising, then drain and place in shade for a day. Water from the top will simply run down the sides of the pot and out through the drainage holes. If, for any reason, the compost is waterlogged, repot the plant in fresh, dry compost and place in shade for a few days, to recover.

SOIL, POTTING COMPOSTS AND POTS

In the garden, any ordinary, not-too-rich, well drained soil is fine, preferably neutral or slightly acid rather than alkaline. Ideally, dig over the bed in winter, adding well-rotted organic matter and removing all weeds.

For container growing, use peat- or loam-based composts; garden soil is unsuitable. Loam-based composts depend on the quality of the loam, which varies; however they are easier to water, contain more food and are heavier and thus more stable. John Innes No. 2 or its equivalent is best. Peat-based products (or vermiculite or perlite equivalents) are standardized, but contain fewer nutrients. They hold more water than loam-based types and thus can get waterlogged, but are difficult to wet once dry. On the other hand, their light weight makes them ideal for hanging baskets. You can mix both types, half and half by bulk, for a good compromise. Some growers mix horticultural coarse sand or grit, ¼ part by bulk, to ¾ parts loam-based compost.

Pots can be plastic or clay. Plastic pots are cheaper, lighter weight and easier to clean, and more practical if you are growing many plants. Clay pots are more expensive, but more stable. Many people find them more attractive, but they absorb water from the compost and dry out faster than plastic pots. Both types of pot need drainage holes.

POTTING UP, POTTING ON AND REPOTTING

For potting up new cuttings and open-grown plants, and for moving strongly growing plants into the next size of pot, it is safer to choose pots just slightly larger than the root ball. In much larger pots, the compost not penetrated by roots is liable to go sour, unless very carefully watered. An 8cm (3½in) pot is fine for a rooted cutting, and as the final pot for miniature zonal types. A 12.5–15cm (5–6in) final pot is fine

POTTING UP AND POTTING ON

1 A well-rooted cutting ready for potting up.

2 Use a small, well-crocked pot, setting the plant at the same soil level it was before.
Firm and water lightly.

3 When roots fill the pot, move young plants on to slightly larger pots. This is normally done in spring.

4 Carefully remove the rootball and prise out any crocks trapped in the roots. Plant at the same level as before, in a well crocked, slightly larger pot, filled with fresh potting compost.

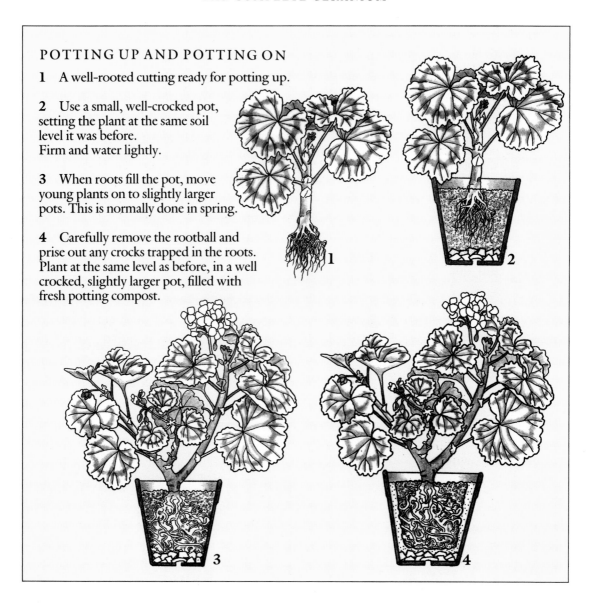

for most types; few need larger than 20cm (8in) pots, although mature regal types may need up to 30cm (12in) pots. As a general rule, flowering is best in pot-bound plants.

For drainage in clay pots, place a layer of broken clay flower pots, or crocks, in the bottom; plastic pots do not need 'crocking'. Place the plant centrally and at the right level, then pour the compost into the pot, around the roots. Leave space between the surface of the compost and pot rim for watering. When full, tap the pot once or twice against the side of a table, to settle the compost, then water lightly and shade for a day or so.

Once the roots fill the pot, pot on. (You can check the drainage holes for signs of roots or, with plastic pots, gently up-end the pot, look at the root ball, and return it if not ready. Potting on is usually done in spring and summer, during the growing season, into pots 2.5–5cm (1–2in) larger than the previous one. The method is the same as for potting up, but with plants in clay pots, check for crocks caught in the root ball and gently prise any out.

At the start of the growing season, gently remove fully grown plants from their pots, use your fingers to tease the compost from the roots and, using fresh compost, repot each one in its old pot. Pruning it at the same time helps balance any accidental loss of root and hastens recovery.

MAKING MORE

Geraniums are easy to root from softwood cuttings, a technique that ensures plants are identical to the parent and, as young plants usually flower best, provides a quick and reliable display of colour. Early spring and late summer are the best time to take cuttings, but any time in spring, summer and early autumn is fine. The early cuttings flower that summer; late cuttings produce larger plants for flowering the following summer.

Select a healthy, ideally non-flowering, shoot; otherwise pinch off any flowers or buds. To take a cutting, use a scalpel or sharp knife – secateurs may crush the shoots. Cut off the shoot 7.5–10cm (3–4in) long, half that for miniatures, cutting just above a leaf joint, or node. Trim the cutting to just below a node, then carefully remove the lower leaves and scales at the base of the leaf stalks. Most geraniums root easily; hormone rooting powder is unnecessary and can actually harm the cuttings.

Use a pencil or finger to make a hole 2.5cm(1in) deep in pots or trays of peat-based seed/cutting compost, or a mixture of equal parts, by bulk, of sharp sand and peat. Use 7.5cm(3in) pots for individual cuttings, or a 12.5cm(5in) pot, for up to five cuttings, inserted round the sides, where drainage is best. Gently insert the cuttings, firm and water very lightly, but do not cover or

MAKING MORE

1   Take 7.5–10 cm (3–4 in) cuttings of sturdy, short-jointed, non-flowering shoots.

2   Remove the lower leaves and scales at the base of the leaf stalks.

3   Make a hole with a pencil or finger, then gently insert the cutting.

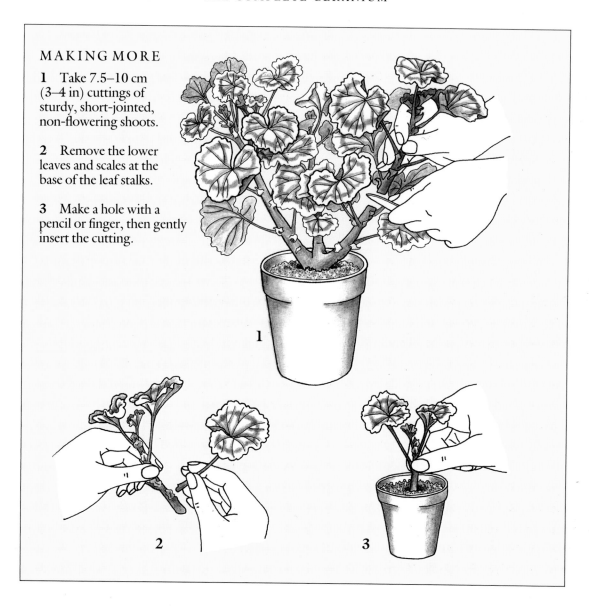

they will be vulnerable to botrytis.

Keep the cuttings warm and shaded from direct sun. 16°C(60°F) is ideal, but if you can provide bottom heat, such as from a heated propagator, the air temperature can be cooler and results will still be good. Keep the compost dryish but water lightly if the cuttings show signs of wilting. Try not to get water on the plants. Rooting can take as little as three days, but longer in cool temperatures and for regal types. Once roots form, new top growth appears, and the cutting will remain firm if gently tugged. Pot up individually those which have been rooted several to a pot.

You can also grow geraniums from seed, especially F_1 and F_2 hybrid strains and ivy-leaved types. In late winter or early spring, sow thinly in pots or trays of seed compost and, again, do not cover. Maintain a steady temperature of at least 21°C(70°F); fluctuations in temperature can delay germination. This normally takes 3–21 days. Once the seedlings are large enough to handle, prick out 7.5cm (3in) apart into trays, or plant individually in 7.5cm (3in) pots of peat or loam-based potting compost. Pot on, as necessary, or plant outdoors after the last frost.

PINCHING OUT AND PRUNING
Many young geraniums, especially zonal, scented-leaved and ivy-leaved types, naturally form a single, unbranched stem unless the tip is nipped, or 'pinched', off, using the thumb and first finger, when the plant is about 10–15cm (4–6in) high. This encourages side shoots to form. Pinching out growing tips should be done continually until a plant's framework is fully formed; with mature plants, it should be done during the growing season. The more you pinch out, the more side shoots form, the better the shape of the plant and the more it flowers. Remember, though, that pinching out also delays flowering. If you intend to

Pinching out:
To encourage side shoots to form, pinch out the growing tip of newly rooted cuttings, and continue pinching out regularly.

Port Carling
Public Library

show your plants, or want them for summer display, allow six weeks from the time of pinching out until flowering.

When pruning, always use sharp, clean secateurs, and cut to just above a node. In autumn, prune back bedding plants potted up for winter by one third. This balances any root loss, and is also economical in terms of space needed. Bushy, mature plants not pruned in autumn are normally pruned, again by one third, in early spring. If you have a 'leggy' plant, with lanky, largely leafless stems, you can prune it by up to three quarters to its benefit, in spring or summer.

OVERWINTERING GERANIUMS

In mild areas, by the sea, or in exceptionally mild winters, geraniums may survive a winter outdoors. This is also true in urban areas, which are usually a little warmer than equivalent rural ones. If you do not want to risk it, take cuttings in late summer and place them in a shady spot to root. Try to choose shoots that leave the mother plant well balanced and attractive, to continue its display value. Just before the first frost, bring the cuttings indoors and discard the old plants.

Alternatively, you can lift all plants, cut them back by one third and pot up individually or insert several in a larger pot or box of barely damp peat. You can use the prunings to make more plants; wait until next spring and take cuttings from the new growth; or simply re-use the old plants – generally least satisfactory as they get older, woodier and less floriferous (regals are an exception, and improve in flowering, up to three years old).

PESTS AND DISEASES

Pests and diseases can cause problems, but the sooner you identify the cause and treat them, the more effective the treatment is. Always inspect a new geranium before buying or introducing it to your house or garden.

With any chemicals, always follow manufacturers' instructions concerning amounts, application method and timing, for maximum benefit and for safety. Always store chemicals well out of reach of children, and never use geraniums that have been treated with chemicals in cooking recipes.

Systemic insecticides tend to be most effective, but you can use natural plant extract insecticides, such as derris, or biological controls – predatory fungi or insects introduced to destroy specific pests in a greenhouse. Unfortunately, biological controls need high minimum temperatures to be effective, they die out as they become successful and must be reintroduced, and may also be incompatible with chemical controls used for other problems.

Blackleg Black, rotting stem bases, especially of cuttings, are caused by a fungus, usually as a result of overwatering or using non-sterile potting compost or dirty pots. Throw out the plant, reduce watering and keep conditions clean.

Botrytis This fungus is most troublesome in cool, damp conditions, especially in a greenhouse in late autumn or winter. Fluffy grey growth on the leaves and stems is the main symptom. Throw out badly infected plants. For slightly infected plants, remove infected leaves, spray with fungicide, reduce watering and increase ventilation and heat. Overcrowded, dead or dying plant material is most vulnerable, so inspect and clean up plants regularly, and space them well apart.

Rust This is very common on zonal types and appears as pale spots on the leaves, with corresponding rust-coloured spots underneath. Cut off the infected leaves and spray with fungicide.
  Buying infected plants is the main source, so caveat emptor!

Yellow leaves Occasional yellow leaves occur naturally, and should be picked off. If all the leaves turn yellow round the edges, but remain firm, underwatering is the likely cause. If they turn yellow and wilt, overwatering may well be the problem.

Non-flowering This can be due to lack of light or heat, excessively rich nitrates or possibly old age.

Red leaf edges This is caused by sudden temperature drops, but the original colour soon returns. Zonal types are especially affected.

Oedema This causes unsightly brown, corky patches on the leaf undersides, especially of ivy-leaved types in spring. It is not contagious, so remove affected leaves and reduce watering.

Aphids These sap-sucking, usually wingless, blue or green insects weaken and disfigure plants and spread viral diseases. The sticky honeydew they secrete is unsightly and encourages sooty mould. Treat with insecticide.

Caterpillars Hand pick and destroy, or treat with insecticide.

Whitefly These tiny, moth-like, sap-sucking, greenhouse pests are found on the leaf underside, especially of regal types. Treat with insecticide or spray with dilute washing-up liquid, which removes their waxy coating. You can also hang up sticky, flypaper-like tags, especially designed to attract whitefly; gently shaking the plant to dislodge the insects helps.

Virus This is spread by sap-sucking insects. Symptoms are mottled, yellow-spotted, distorted or crinkled leaves, especially in winter and early spring. There is no cure, so destroy plants as soon as seen, to prevent further infection.

SEASONAL GUIDE TO CARING FOR GERANIUMS

SPRING

○ Increase watering and start feeding, as the weather warms up. Use a balanced or high nitrate fertilizer to start with, switching to a high potassium feed in late spring.

○ Prune potted plants back by one third in early spring, if you have not done so in autumn, and use the prunings as cuttings. Continue taking cuttings through spring.

○ Sow seeds in early spring and pot up seedlings when large enough to handle.

○ Start potting on and repotting in early spring, and continue through spring.

○ Provide heat, if frost threatens.

○ Order plants from geranium specialists in early spring, while the choice is still good.

○ Pinch out growing tips and check regularly for pests and diseases.

○ On warm, sunny days, put plants outdoors to harden off. Bring in at night. After the last frost, move pots outdoors or plant in the open ground.

○ Give plants on a window sill a quarter turn every few days, to prevent lopsided growth.

○ Provide extra ventilation for plants under glass on warm days.

SUMMER

○ Continue taking, inspecting and potting up cuttings.

○ Continue pinching out.

○ Continue feeding, using a high potassium fertilizer, and watering plants regularly.

○ Continue checking for pests or diseases, and spraying as necessary.

○ Apply shading in hot, sunny weather. Continue ventilating and damp down the greenhouse as necessary.

○ Give plants on a window sill a quarter turn every few days, to prevent lopsided growth.

○ Remove faded flowers and leaves.

Autumn

○ Lift and pot up or otherwise store open grown plants to be overwintered before the first frost. Move in potted geraniums.

○ Cut plants back, and use cuttings for propagation.

○ Begin decreasing feeding and watering as the weather turns cooler. In mid-autumn, stop feeding and reduce watering to the minimum.

○ Continue checking for pests and diseases, and spray as necessary.

○ Give plants on a window sill a quarter turn every few days, to prevent lopsided growth.

○ Make sure greenhouse and window glass is clean. Insulate the greenhouse, if necessary.

○ Remove faded flowers and leaves.

○ Provide heat if frost threatens.

○ Provide ventilation, weather permitting, or use a fan.

Winter

○ Water sparingly.

○ Continue checking for pests and diseases, and spray as necessary.

○ Provide heat, if frost threatens.

○ Continue ventilating, weather permitting, or use a fan.

○ Give plants on a window sill a quarter turn every few days, to prevent lopsided growth.

○ Remove faded flowers and leaves.

○ In mild weather, dig over next summer's outdoor beds, removing all weeds and adding organic matter.

○ Send for specialist geranium nursery catalogues.

○ Sow seeds.

APPENDIX

GERANIUMS AND PELARGONIUMS
The Main Differences

The Geraniaceae family of plants includes five genera of which Pelargonium and Geranium are the best known. There are two main differences between the two: first, pelargoniums have zygomorphic flowers – ie their petals and sepals are dissimilar in size and shape and are arranged symmetrically on one plane, rather like a vertical mirror image or butterfly – while geraniums have actimorphic flowers – ie petals and sepals of similar size and shape, arranged radially, rather like those of a buttercup. Modern hybridizers, however, have 'improved' the irregular flower form of pelargoniums, and many, especially zonal varieties, carry blooms that appear perfectly symmetrical and round. The second, more technical, difference is that geraniums have ten fertile stamens, while pelargoniums have no more than seven fertile stamens out of ten.

TYPES OF GERANIUMS

This brief selection gives some idea of the variety available, in addition to the types pictured on pages 10–21.

ZONALS

Single

Snowstorm	white
Paul Crampel	scarlet bedder
Loveliness	pinkish-lilac
Rachel Fischer	white-eyed, cerise-pink

Semi-double

Always	pink flushed white
Hyfield's Ballerina	red-orange
Baronne de Rothschild	pale pink
Shocking	bright pink
Hermione	white
Genetrix	carmine-rose
Radiance	white-eyed, coral-red

Miniature

Royal Norfolk	wine-red, double
Frills	quilled, coral-pink
Delta	neon-pink, double
Snowbaby	large-flowered, white
Anna	white-eyed mauve, single

Dwarf

Eclipse	salmon flowers, nearly black leaves
China Doll	salmon flowers, dark leaves
Fantasie	white, double
Golden Orf	coral flowers, yellow & bronze leaves

Ornamental-leaved

Tricoloured

Mr (or Mrs) Henry Cox	yellow leaf with deep red overlaid, green/black butterfly centre; pale salmon-pink flowers
Dolly Varden	creamy white leaf margin, rosy red zone, sage-green butterfly centre; single vermilion flowers

Bicoloured

Mrs Quilter	golden yellow-bronzed leaf; salmon pink flowers
Flowers of Spring	silver-edged green leaf; scarlet flowers
Happy Thought	yellow-centred green leaf; red flowers
Chelsea Gem	silvery green, white-edged leaf; double light pink flowers
Freak of Nature	white, wavy leaf with irregular green margin; single scarlet flowers

Coloured

Hunter's Moon	golden leaf; single orange flowers
Golden Lilac Mist	golden leaf; pale lilac flowers
Red Black Vesuvius	bronze-black leaf; single scarlet flowers

Deacon/Floribunda

Deacon Arlon	green-centred white
Deacon Sunburst	brilliant orange
Deacon Picotee	purple-stained white
Deacon Finale	deep burgundy

Irenes

Modesty	double, white
Penny	neon-pink, white-eyed
Kathleen Gamble	salmon
Regina	pink
King of Denmark	salmon
Treasure Chest	orange-scarlet

Rosebud/Noisette

Pink Rambler; Plum Rambler; Scarlet Rambler; Red Rambler	self-descriptive colours
Rosebud Supreme	blood-red flowers

Cactus-flowered (Poinsettia Geraniums)

Coronia	single pink
Noel	double white
Attraction	pink and coral striped
Tangerine	double orange
Fire Dragon	single, scarlet

Stellar

Stellar Red Devil	scarlet
Stellar Arctic Star	white
Stellar Salmon	salmon-pink
Stellar Cathay	salmon-pink, white-eyed
Super Nora	frilly, lilac pink
Gemini	pink, white-centred
Golden Staph	orange-red flowers, yellow leaves

F_1 and F_2 hybrids

Ringo; Disco; Pulsar; Orbit; Carefree; Sprinter	seed strains with different colours
Mustang	brilliant scarlet
Cherry glow	cerise
Cherie	blush-pink, salmon
Bright Eyes	red, white-eyed

REGALS Lady/Martha Washington (P. × domesticum)

Aztec	large white, pinky red splashes, veined maroon; compact, free flowering
Fringed Aztec	as above with fringed petals
Black Magic	nearly black
Braque	fuchsia pink, shaded lavender
Cezanne	royal purple, white underside
Georgia Peach	apricot pink
Grand Slam	rose-red petals with dark markings; compact bushy growth
Hazel Cherry	cherry red, near black blotches
Birthday Girl	orchid pink, feathered magenta
Pink Bonanza	pale salmon; compact, long-flowering

Miniature/Dwarf/Angel

Catford Belle	pale & deep purple
Moon Maiden	soft lilac
Mme Layal	purple & white
Tip-Top Duet	lower petals mauve, upper petals maroon

Uniques

Crimson Unique	
White Unique	purple veined
Purple Unique	
Rollinson's Unique	magenta/purple; rose scented
Voodoo	velvety red and black
Scarlet Unique	highly aromatic

IVY LEAVED (P. peltatum)

Amethyst	semi double, pale purple
Crocodile	magenta pink, creamy white veined leaves
Mexican Beauty	dark red
Patricia	double, pale lilac
Yale	semi double, rich red
Santa Paula	double mauve

Harlequin

Harlequin Mahogany	reddish brown edges to white petals
Harlequin Pretty Girl	orange & white
Harlequin Picotee	candy-pink edges to white petals
Harlequin Alpine Glow	cerise edges to cerise and white streaked petals

Miniature and Dwarf

Gay Baby	mauve & white
Sugar Baby	pink
Gay Baby	double candy pink
Flakey	lilac & white

CLUBS AND SOCIETIES

British Pelargonium and
Geranium Society
Hon Sec, Mr Ron and Mrs Carol
Helyar
134 Montrose Avenue
Welling
Kent, UK
DA16 2QY

The Geraniaceae Society
Membership Secretary, R. Clifton
7 Crabble Road
Dover
Kent, UK
CT17 0QD

Australian Geranium Society
Hon Sec, Mrs Grace Perry
118 Thornley Road
Fairfield West
New South Wales 2165

International Geranium Society
Mrs Robin Schultz
4610 Druid Street
Los Angeles,
California USA 90032

South African Pelargonium and
Geranium Society
Mrs J. de Villiers
107 Silwood Road
Bramley Gardens
2090 S.A.

NURSERIES

UK

The Vernon Geranium Nursery
Cuddington Way
Cheam, Sutton
Surrey SM2 7JB

Beckwood Nurseries
New Inn Road
Beckley, nr Oxford
Oxfordshire OX3 9SS

Clifton Geranium Nursery
Cherry Orchard Road
Whyke, Chichester
West Sussex PO19 2BX

Thorp's Nurseries
257 Finchampstead Road
Wokingham, Berkshire
RH11 3JT

Fibrex Nurseries Ltd
Honeybourne Road
Pebworth
Stratford on Avon
Warwick CV37 8XT

SOUTH AFRICA

Charles Craib
P.O. Box 67142
2021 Bryanston
South Africa

Parsley's Cape Seeds
P.O. Box 1375
Somerset West 7130
South Africa

USA

Logee's Greenhouse
141 North Street
Danielson, CT 06239
(203) 774 – 8038

Fischer Geraniums
24500 Southwest 167th Ave
Homestead, Fla 33031
(305) 245 – 9464
fax: (305) 245 – 9474

Shady Hill
821 Walnut Street
Batavia, IL 60510
(708) 879 – 5665

Davidson-Wilson Greenhouses
Route 2, Box 168
Crawfordsville,
IN 47933 – 9423
(317) 364 – 0556
fax: (317) 364 – 0563

Cook's Geranium Nursery
712 North Grand
Highway 14 North
Lyons, KA 67554
(316) 257 5033

Oglevee, Ltd
150 Oglevee Lane
Connellsville, PA 15425
(412) 628 – 8360

CANADA

Colonial Florists, Ltd
58 Broadway Avenue
St Catherine's
Ontario L2MIM4
(416) 934 – 3196
fax: (416) 646 – 7100

INDEX

ACKNOWLEDGMENTS

A-Z Botanical Collection   18
Biofotos   7, 14(L), 34, 36
Boys Syndication   43 (Michael Boys); 28(R), 29,
    31, 32 (Jacqui Hurst)
Breslich & Foss   53, 73 (Jacqui Hurst); 51, 55,
    56–7, 63, 67, 69, 70 (Debbie Patterson)
Christie's Colour Library   10, 44, 72, front cover
Elizabeth Whiting & Associates   6, 26–7, 30, 39,
    45, 46

Fine Art Photographics   9, 22, 38, 46, 60
Garden Picture Library   11 (top R, Brian Carter), 15
    (R, J S Sira), 21 (L, Brian Carter), 23, 24 (Brigitte
    Thomas), 28 (L, David Russell), 40–41 (John
    Glover)
Harry Smith Photographic Collection   11 (L, bot-
    tom R), 12, 13, 14 (R), 15 (R), 16 (all), 17, 19
    (both), 20, 21 (top & bottom R), 33, 35, 42, 47
Visual Arts   49